TOUR DE FRANCE

GLOBAL CITIZENS: SPORTS

Published in the United States of America by Cherry Lake Publishing
Ann Arbor, Michigan
www.cherrylakepublishing.com

Content Adviser: Liv Williams, Editor, www.iLivExtreme.com
Reading Adviser: Marla Conn, MS, Ed., Literacy specialist, Read-Ability, Inc.

Photo Credits: ©sezer66/Shutterstock, cover, 1; ©Istomina Olena/Shutterstock, 5; ©Radu Razvan/Shutterstock,
6, 11, 16, 23, 25, 26; ©Frederic Legrand - COMEO/Shutterstock, 7, 28; ©Everett Historical/Shutterstock, 9;
©Ahmed Akl/Shutterstock, 13; ©Huw Fairclough/Shutterstock, 15; ©Alexander Gordeyev/Shutterstock, 19;
©Jan de Wild/Shutterstock, 20; ©ricochet64/Shutterstock, 22

Library of Congress Cataloging-in-Publication Data

Names: Hellebuyck, Adam, author. | Deimel, Laura, author.
Title: Tour de France / written by Adam Hellebuyck and Laura Deimel.
Description: Ann Arbor, Michigan : Cherry Lake Publishing, [2019] | Series: Global Citizens: Sports |
    Audience: Grades 4 to 6 | Includes bibliographical references and index.
Identifiers: LCCN 2019004217 | ISBN 9781534147522 (hardcover) | ISBN 9781534150386 (paperback) |
    ISBN 9781534148956 (pdf) | ISBN 9781534151819 (hosted ebook)
Subjects: LCSH: Tour de France (Bicycle race)—History—Juvenile literature.
Classification: LCC GV1049.2.T68 .H45 2019 | DDC 796.6/20944—dc23
LC record available at https://lccn.loc.gov/2019004217

Cherry Lake Publishing would like to acknowledge the work of the Partnership for 21st Century Learning.
Please visit *www.p21.org* for more information.

Printed in the United States of America
Corporate Graphics

ABOUT THE AUTHORS

Laura Deimel is a fourth grade teacher and Adam Hellebuyck is a high school social studies
teacher at University Liggett School in Grosse Pointe Woods, Michigan. They have worked
together for the past 8 years and are thrilled they could combine two of their passions, reading
and sports, into this work.

TABLE OF CONTENTS

History: Then to Now

The Tour de France is the most famous men's bicycle race in the world. Riders come from all around to participate in this challenging 21-day race. It has risen in popularity since its founding in 1903. While there were only 60 riders that first year, in 2018 176 riders from 30 different countries competed in the race.

Origins of the Tour de France

In 1903, the editors of the sports newspaper *L'Auto* wanted to increase the paper's **circulation**. One of the most popular sports in France at that time was bicycle racing. The editor

The 1926 Tour de France was the longest in history.
It totaled 3,570 miles (5,745 kilometers).

The shortest stage in the first Tour de France was 167 miles (268 km). This was far longer than the longest stage in the 2018 race, which was only 144 miles (231 km).

Each year, the Tour de France uses a different route.
But the race always finishes in Paris, France.

of *L'Auto* was a famous French cyclist named Henri Desgrange.
Desgrange and his staff decided to hold a bicycle race around
France to boost sales of the newspaper.

The first Tour de France started on July 1, 1903, and took place
over six stages. Each stage ranged from 167 miles (268 km) to
293 miles (471 km) long over mainly flat **terrain**. The race was
a huge success and helped raise the popularity of *L'Auto*. Sales of
the newspaper rose from 20,000 a day in 1903 to over 850,000
a day at its highest in 1933.

Challenges in the Race

Holding such a long bicycle race at that time posed many challenges. No one could watch all the riders along the whole course, so some riders would cheat and take shortcuts along the route. Other riders were attacked on the route, just to keep them from winning! In order to cut down on cheating, the organizers ended night riding in 1904. They also shortened the distance of each stage, but added more stages. Today's Tour de France consists of 21 stages covering about 2,200 miles (3,500 km) over a 23-day period. This made it possible for each cyclist to be seen through more of the race.

The Tour de France has been held continuously since it began 1903, with two exceptions. The races were canceled when France fought in World War I and again during World War II.

Challenging Fans

Riders still face some challenges from fans today. As recently as 2004, cyclists complained of fans threatening them along one of the routes near the Alpine Mountains.

The Tour de France in 1940 was canceled because of World War II.

Some people volunteer during the race to act as guides for the fans visiting.
Their official title is Tour Maker.

The Most Watched Sporting Event in the World

Over 12 million people watch the Tour de France in person, making it the most watched sporting event in the world. This is because the course travels along highways and city streets, and there is no cost to line the sides of the roads to watch the competitors. In addition, according to some media sources, over 3.5 billion people watch some part of the 21-day event on television each year!

Developing Questions

While almost all riders are honest and hardworking, there are some examples of riders in the Tour de France cheating throughout its history. Make a list of all the ways you think cyclists could cheat in the race. Based on your understanding of the Tour de France, what could you do to prevent cheating from happening? How could you encourage cyclists not to cheat?

CHAPTER 2

Geography: The World Participates

While the Tour de France takes place primarily in France, and has had many French riders and fans, people from all around the world participate in the race. Millions more from many different countries watch the race in person, on television, or online.

The Riders

In the first Tour de France in 1903, 80 percent of the cyclists were French. Over time, more riders from other countries joined the race. In 2018, only 20 percent of the riders were French. However, France is still the country with the most riders in

Despite its name, the Tour de France has stages covering other countries, from Belgium and Corsica to the Netherlands and Germany.

the race. To compare, 6 percent of riders came from Australia, 3 percent came from the United States, and 2 percent came from South Africa and Ethiopia.

France is also the most successful country in the Tour de France. A French rider has won the race 36 times in its history. France has won the Tour de France twice as many times as the second-place country, Belgium. Riders from Belgium have won the race 18 times.

The Viewers

People around the world read about or watch the Tour de France. In 2012, 20 percent of the world's population followed or watched the race. In 2015, that number increased to 23 percent. While France hosts the event each year, the race's viewership in that country has actually gone down over the past few years. Only 32 percent of people in France say they watch the race each year. The countries with the highest viewership are the Netherlands and Spain. About 38 percent of people in these countries say they follow the Tour de France each year.

Tour de France Outside of Europe

While France and Belgium have won the race many times, there are many countries that have never won the race. The only countries outside of Europe that have ever won the race are the United States and Australia!

Of the top 10 winners in the 2018 Tour de France, only one was from France! Everyone else was from Great Britain, the Netherlands, Slovenia, Spain, Ireland, Russia, and Columbia.

Watching in Person

While most fans who watch the Tour de France from the side of the road are from France, the race organizers believe that 20 percent of fans come from all over the world. They have a hard time collecting that data because the Tour de France is one of the few sports where fans do not need to purchase a ticket to watch it live!

About 20 percent of roadside spectators aren't from France.

Traveling to watch the race from another country can be a challenge. Fans may not know where to stay, where to eat, or even when to arrive to see the cyclists go by. However, there are travel agents in France who specialize in bringing people from other countries to watch the race. They help find these fans great lodging and restaurants, and even arrange their transportation from town to town to watch the riders.

Gathering and Evaluating Sources

*To travel over 2,000 miles (3,219 km), a cyclist needs to pedal a lot! The average rider pedals 90 **revolutions** each minute and pushes the pedals over 486,000 times during the entire race. Cyclists burn around 4,500 calories each day in order to pedal this much. Think about all the things you do in a day. How many calories does each activity burn? Using your local library and trusted sources on the internet, try to figure out how many calories you burn in a day.*

CHAPTER 3

Civics:
Follow the Rules

Since the Tour de France is such a long race, there are many rules that cyclists are expected to follow. There are also many ways for them to earn **accolades** during the Tour de France.

Rules of the Road

Many of the race's **regulations** are designed to keep riders safe. For example, all riders are required to wear helmets throughout the entire Tour de France. In addition, riders must always have their race numbers visible during each stage of the race. There are also rules for the riders' **caravan** of vehicles. Since the race is so long, cyclists need people in cars and on

At the end of each stage, the person to cross the finish line first is called the stage winner.

Fabian Cancellara holds the record for wearing the yellow jersey for more days than any other rider without winning the Tour de France.

motorcycles to provide them with food, water, or medical attention if they need it. Specific rules address when a rider can get something from a vehicle and how close the vehicles can get to the cyclists.

Another rule that has been a tradition since the beginning of the Tour de France involves riders' signatures. Cyclists must sign in at the beginning of each stage, and if they don't they could be fined $85. While the signatures themselves are not important to the race, the signature ceremony is important so fans can see the cyclists at the starting line.

Colorful Jerseys

The Tour de France rules award cyclists with jerseys for accomplishing certain **feats** during the race. Riders can earn jerseys in four ways: if they are the fastest overall rider, the rider with the most points, the fastest mountain climber, or the fastest young rider.

The fastest overall rider in each stage of the race earns the right to wear the yellow jersey, called *maillot jaune* in French, in the next stage. This is the most well-known symbol of victory in the Tour de France, and it's the jersey every rider wants the opportunity to wear. The green jersey, or *maillot vert*, is given

Developing Claims and Using Evidence

The Tour de France is an uncommon race because it provides jerseys, accolades, and money for more than just the cyclist who finishes first at the end. Why do you think that the organizers of the race did this? What are the advantages of this system? What are the disadvantages? Use the evidence you find from the library or the internet to support your claims.

If you were going to organize a race of your own through your local community, what categories would you give jerseys in? What would those jerseys look like and why?

There are rare occasions where a rider can wear a yellow jersey,
but not have won a stage.

There were 190 countries around the world that televised the 2018 Tour de France.

to the rider with the most points at the end of each stage. Points can be awarded for winning or placing in stages, or for winning shorter sprints within a stage. This is sometimes called the "sprinter's jersey." The polka-dot jersey, or *maillot à pois rouges*, is awarded to the rider who climbs to the **crest** of mountains in the fastest time. This rider is usually called the "king of the mountains." The white jersey, or *maillot blanc*, is given to the fastest young rider under the age of 26.

CHAPTER 4

Economics: It's a Team Effort

Many people must work together in order to make the Tour de France a success. Riders must work within a team in order to have the best chance of winning the race. Organizers must work together with businesses and other groups to raise money. Mayors and city officials must work together if they want to host the Grand Départ at the beginning of the race.

Teams on the Tour

While a lot of attention is given to the speedy cyclists who win the race, they have an entire team of people who help them be successful. Cyclists compete on teams of eight. Each team has a leader that is supported and protected by the remaining riders. The cyclists on a team each have a specific task. Some cyclists

The overall winner of the 2018 Tour de France was awarded $582,000. But this prize money was to be shared among the other riders and crew.

ride in front of their leader to help block the wind. This keeps the leader from having to pedal as hard. There are also teammates who make sure the leader has enough food and water. Teams also have groups following the cyclists, such as mechanics, cooks, and doctors. They make sure the riders and bicycles are kept in great condition. Teams spend a lot of money to build a strong group of cyclists with the best chance of winning the race. Teams need to train together and practice often so they can work as one unit.

Some advertising caravans go all out!

The Advertising Caravan

All the money to run the Tour de France first came from *L'Auto*, the newspaper that started the race. When the paper went out of business in 1947, race organizers worried that they would not be able to raise enough money to run the race anymore. The organizers came up with a creative solution. They would give businesses a chance to advertise their products during the race

Taking Informed Action

Being a member of a cycling team in the Tour de France is a great achievement. As you have read, there are many different jobs for riders on each team. There are also many jobs for the people who support the riders. Take a look at all these different jobs on one of the team's websites. What job would you most like to have on a racing team? Would you like to ride or help in another way? How could you reach this goal?

Riders in Tour de France teams also earn a salary. Chris Froome, team leader, makes about $3.9 million a year, while the other riders earn about $180,000 to $550,000.

in an advertising caravan. This is a group of cars that have advertisements on the side. The caravan would drive in front of the **peloton** of racers, where fans along the road could see them. People would also hand out samples of their products from the advertising caravan. This helped earn these businesses a lot of money. People were more likely to buy the products advertised in the Tour de France.

[21ST CENTURY SKILLS LIBRARY]

Bidding for the Grand Départ

Many cities have **bid** to host the Grand Départ for the Tour de France. The city that starts the race can earn a lot of **revenue** from fans wanting to be there for it. For example, when the race began in Yorkshire, England, in 2014, almost 5 million fans were in attendance. All of these people stayed in hotels, ate in restaurants, and spent money in the city on other entertainment. The county made nearly $163 million just for hosting the start of the race. Since people in more than 190 countries around the world watch part of the Tour de France, either in person or on television, hosting the Grand Départ can also mean more tourists for years to come.

Communicating Conclusions

According to Tour de France officials, nearly half of the world's population, or about 3.8 billion people, watch the Tour de France, either live in person or on-screen. Do you think this data for the Tour de France is accurate? Why or why not? Share your thoughts with friends and family. Ask them what they think.

Think About It

Cyclists from 13 different countries have won the Tour de France. Some countries have won more times than others. Study the information in the table below about how many times riders from certain countries have won the race. What do you notice? Why do you think that some countries have had more winners than others? Does geography make an impact on which countries produce winning cyclists? What evidence can you find to back up your idea?

Country	Tour de France Wins
France	36
Belgium	18
Spain	12
Italy	10
United Kingdom	6
Luxembourg	5
United States	3
Netherlands, Switzerland	2
Denmark, Germany, Ireland	1

[21ST CENTURY SKILLS LIBRARY]

For More Information

Further Reading

Hamilton, S. L. *Tour de France.* Minneapolis, MN: ABDO Publishing Company, 2013.

Moore, Tim. *French Revolutions: Cycling the Tour de France.* New York, NY: St. Martins Griffin, 2003.

Websites

Le Tour
https://www.letour.fr/en
Learn more about the Tour de France on the official website.

Sports Illustrated Kids—13 Things You Need to Know About the Tour de France
https://www.sikids.com/si-kids/2016/01/12/tour-de-france-13-things-you-know
Read interesting facts about cycling's most famous race.

GLOSSARY

accolades (AK-uh-laydz) awards or honors

bid (BID) made a proposal

caravan (KAR-uh-van) a group of people traveling together

circulation (sur-kyuh-LAY-shuhn) the number of people who purchase and read a news source

crest (KREST) the top of a mountain

feats (FEETS) achievements or accomplishments

peloton (peh-leh-TAHN) the main body of riders in a bicycle race

regulations (reg-yuh-LAY-shuhnz) rules to follow

revenue (REV-uh-noo) money received for work

revolutions (rev-uh-LOO-shuhnz) full circles

terrain (tuh-RAYN) land

INDEX

[21ST CENTURY SKILLS LIBRARY]